THE NEW YORKER IN WESTPORT

BY EVE POTTS AND ANDREW BENTLEY

The New Yorker in Westport by Eve Potts and Andrew Bentley
Copyright © 2015, Westport Historical Society

All images licensed by Condé Nast to the Westport Historical Society for the express purpose of this book. All rights reserved.

No part of this book may be used or reproduced in any manner whatsoever without prior written permission of the Westport Historical Society, except in the case of brief quotations for reviews.

ISBN 978-1-4951-4420-2

Book & cover design by Andrew Bentley
Cover image by Albert Hubbell

Printed in China by ArtBookPrinting.Com, Grand Rapids, Michigan

ACKNOWLEDGMENTS

Many people contributed to making this book a reality including Westporters Nina Bentley, Richard Bentley, Miggs Burroughs, Katie Chase, Dorothy Curran, Helen Klisser During, Fiona Garland, Mark Potts, Joyce Thompson, and Dan Woog. Also contributing were Edward F. Gerber, President of the Westport Historical Society, and Woody Klein, author of the book *Westport Connecticut; The Story of a New England Town's Rise to Prominence*, as well as the folks at Condé Nast.

Most importantly, we salute the artists whose work this book celebrates: Charles Addams, Perry Barlow, Whitney Darrow Jr., James Daugherty, Edna Eicke, Arthur Getz, Alice Harvey, Helen Hokinson, Albert Hubbell, David Preston, Garrett Price and Charles Saxon.

The publication of this book, a volunteer project of the Westport Historical Society, was made possible by the Potts Book Fund and by matching donations made by Andrew Bentley and Fiona Garland. All funds raised from the sale of the book will be allocated to the Westport Historical Society's operating fund.

INTRODUCTION

The idea for this book was born when long-time Westporter Eve Potts was thumbing through her copy of *The Complete Book of Covers from The New Yorker, 1925-1989* and recognized that the August 20, 1973, cover was of Compo Beach pavilion, a scene she could see from her front porch. A bit of research revealed that the cover was by Albert Hubbell, a Westport artist. Hubbell had lived in Westport for many years and often used local scenes as inspiration for cover illustrations. This led Eve to wonder how many other local artists had also produced *New Yorker* covers. The incredible answer was that 767 covers—enough to fill 14-years' worth of *New Yorkers*—were produced by artists living in and around Westport!

Eve knew that this was not a coincidence and set about finding out why so many local artists had created *New Yorker* covers, the pinnacle of commercial artistic success. She learned that the answer was James Geraghty, art editor of *The New Yorker* from 1939 to 1973. Born in Spokane, Washington, he was working as a freelance writer in New York City when he saw a request for *New Yorker* cartoon ideas. He wrote down a hundred ideas and took them to the editor the next morning. He was soon hired by founder and editor Harold Ross as an "idea man." In time, Geraghty became the magazine's art director, responsible for both the cover art and cartoons.

A few years into the job, when Geraghty and his wife were looking for a good place to raise their children, artist Perry Barlow suggested they come to Westport where a stable of artists, including Alice Harvey and Garrett Price, had already moved. Due to Geraghty's influence and mentoring ways, more artists became attracted to the area. They all became good friends;

they bowled together, they ate together and they worked together. More and more *New Yorker* covers by Westport area artists began to appear, many of them mirroring their suburban commuter lifestyles.

These wonderful discoveries were too good to keep out of the public eye, so in 2014 the Westport Historical Society put on an exhibition called "Cover Story: *The New Yorker* in Westport" curated by Eve Potts with Dorothy Curran. The show was a great success; by far the most popular anyone could remember seeing at the Society's Wheeler House headquarters. A big fan of the show, Fiona Garland suggested that a book should be printed to commemorate the show. Everyone at the Westport Historical Society agreed, but initial attempts to acquire the rights to the images were frustrating. Unwilling to give up on the idea, we set about selecting the best 50 covers. Our lucky break came when we realized that the Historical Society was selling commercially produced *New Yorker* cover puzzles in its gift shop. If the puzzle company could acquire the rights, then we could too. After a few blind alleys, we found our way to the proper department at Condé Nast and were able to secure the rights we needed to proceed with the project.

Over the ensuing months, we reached out to many Westporters—artists, historians, old-timers, business people, writers and anyone who would listen — knitting together stories about our town to go alongside the 50 covers. We hope that we have succeeded in producing a book that Westporters will enjoy for many years to come.

Eve Potts and Andrew Bentley

THE ROARING TWENTIES

Longtime Westport artist James Daugherty illustrated this art-deco-style cover during *The New Yorker's* first year of publication. It was the Jazz Age, peopled by the bright young things who'd lived, fought through and survived World War I. Class and gender distinctions were being slowly erased and women across America were gaining the right to vote, to smoke and to play sports as competitively as the men did.

In the 1920s, Westport was expanding rapidly and bustling with optimism and modernism. It became a cultural beehive, complete with jazzy party-prone flappers with bobbed haircuts and speakeasies that openly defied Prohibition while town officials turned a blind eye.

One of the most popular spots in town was the Miramar nightclub, which later became the Penguin apartments, located on Hillspoint Road just past the railroad bridge where there are now a group of condos. The Miramar drew the fast crowd from the entire New York area, as well as well-known Hollywood guests such as George Raft and James Cagney.

Cover by James Daugherty

GONE BUT NOT FORGOTTEN

This cover appeared at the height of the 1920s boom years, when wealth increased enormously across the United States. During this period, Westport was home to its fair share of grand estates. Edward T. Bedford, a partner of John D. Rockefeller, owned a magnificent beachfront property complete with a half-mile racetrack and horse stables. Morris Ketchum, a powerful Wall Street banker, owned a 500-acre estate called Hockanum on Cross Highway that included extensive flower gardens, a vineyard and a hunting forest. There was also Compo House, a mansion on 23 acres at the corner of the Post Road and North Compo Road that was built by the business tycoon Richard Henry Winslow and later owned by Baron Walter Langer von Langendorff, founder of Evyan perfumes.

It is likely that the rich lady clipping the red roses on this cover lost her butler and her pearls after the stock market crashed in 1929. In Westport, many grand estates were broken up—gone, but not forgotten. Parts of Bedford's estate became a corporate park, now home to one of the world's largest hedge funds. The house at Hockanum is still standing, albeit on only a handful of its original acres. As for Compo House, which was first converted into a sanitarium and later became the Baron's property, the buildings were demolished in 1971. The lush landscaped acreage is now a town-owned park with walking and biking trails and a large off-leash area for dogs.

Cover by Helen Hokinson

BLOWING SMOKE

You would have been laughed off the train in 1933 if you had suggested that smoking should be banned. The men in this car have made a table out of a suitcase so they can play cards and are puffing on cigars, paying no heed to the dear lady seatmate suffering in their midst. Times were tough during the Great Depression, but in spite of pervasive poverty, smokers (men, not women, please) experienced a kind of Golden Age. They smoked outdoors, indoors, in the boardroom, in the bedroom and, as depicted here, on the train to work.

The white-gloved lady on this cover would be most astonished at today's no-smoking laws. Indeed, Westport is well known for its progressive stand as one of the first communities to pass an ordinance that required restaurant owners to segregate smokers from nonsmokers. It's clear that Westporters don't just blow smoke, they make things happen.

Cover by Garrett Price

ENCORE ENCORE

Many famous actors have graced the stage of the Westport Country Playhouse since this *New Yorker* cover. In the 1930s, Lawrence Langner and his wife, Armina Marshall, who had already achieved remarkable success as theater producers, purchased a big red barn in an old Westport apple orchard. They transformed the former 1835 cow barn and subsequent tannery, called the Kemper Leather Works, into a theater. Their enterprise became one of the first summer theaters in the country, over the years featuring many of the most famous actors of their day, including:

Alan Alda	Helen Hayes
Tallulah Bankhead	James Earl Jones
Montgomery Clift	Gene Kelly
Rodney Dangerfield	Jack Klugman
Bette Davis	Liza Minnelli
Kirk Douglas	Marilyn Monroe
Michael Douglas	Robert Redford
Mia Farrow	Jason Robards
Henry Fonda	Jessica Tandy
Jane Fonda	Elizabeth Taylor
Eva Gabor	Marlo Thomas
Zsa Zsa Gabor	Gene Wilder

And, of course, Westport's Paul Newman and Joanne Woodward.

Cover by Helen Hokinson

THE CUSTOMER'S ALWAYS RIGHT

It was 1936 and the Midwest still was mired in dust bowl problems and California was illegally trying to stop unemployed Americans from coming into the state to find work. Meanwhile, Westport was rapidly evolving from a small town of farmers, artisans and shopkeepers into a suburban bedroom community of New York City. Stores such as Charles Food Shop opened up to serve the new arrivals. The jaunty butchers, sporting straw boaters, stood on freshly strewn sawdust serving fussy customers like the one on this *New Yorker* cover.

Today, the old-time Westport businesses have mostly been replaced by high-end chain stores where svelte twenty-somethings stand ready to help picky shoppers decide between dozens of different styles of yoga pants. Then, as now, success on Main Street has always come down to the golden rule of retail: the customer's always right.

Cover by Perry Barlow

COOL HAND LUKE

When this *New Yorker* issue hit the newsstands, Paul Newman and Joanne Woodward were not even teenagers. Nevertheless, there is a resemblance between the young pair with engine trouble and Westport's most celebrated couple.

Newman and Woodward were first introduced to Westport during the making of the 1958 movie *Rally Round the Flag, Boys,* a spoof written by Westporter Max Shulman. The couple, married in 1958, raised their three daughters in a Coleytown-area house and defied Hollywood norms by celebrating their 50th wedding anniversary.

During this time, they made and directed movies, collected Oscars and acted on stage at the Westport Country Playhouse while building an enormous charitable organization. They were active fundraisers and generous with their time and attention to many local Westport organizations.

Cover by Alice Harvey

LEFT AT THE SCARECROW

This *New Yorker* cover presents the charming scene of city dwellers driving through Westport asking directions from a local farming couple. While he is indignant in his certainty, she is confident and composed, leaving little doubt as to whose directions are correct.

This amusing scene is set during the Great Depression, long before the extended postwar economic recovery that made America far wealthier than ever. This greater wealth led many New Yorkers to discover Westport not only as a nice spot to visit on weekends, but also as a place to live fulltime.

One generation later, the gentrification of Westport would get under way in earnest, and we can imagine that the farm pictured here would be sold to a developer and subdivided into spacious single-family homes with gourmet kitchens and two-car garages.

Cover by Perry Barlow

NEXT STOP: WESTPORT

When this couple in top hat, tails and mink coat appeared on the cover of *The New Yorker,* the Great Depression still lingered. A late train back home to Connecticut after an evening in New York City was the affordable option to a chauffeured limousine. The commuter train fascinated Westport artist Perry Barlow; he loved the social contrast of people from quite different personal worlds united by a simple journey.

While President Roosevelt's New Deal had mitigated some effects of the Great Depression by 1938, it did not end the economic crisis entirely. To make matters worse, that same year a powerful hurricane struck the East Coast and Westport with deadly force. In Europe, a much bigger storm was brewing. But when World War II erupted, the American public rallied, and Westporters from every socioeconomic group worked together to support the war effort.

Cover by Perry Barlow

SHE'S NO WALLFLOWER

This domestic scene made the cover of *The New Yorker* long before America's most famous tastemaker, Martha Stewart, moved to Westport in 1971. She bought an antique farmhouse on Turkey Hill Road, opened a gourmet food shop called The Market Basket and quickly became known for her catering skills and unique presentations.

Within a decade she was running a multimillion-dollar business. By 1999, her brand included books, a magazine and a television program and when the company went public on the New York Stock Exchange, Martha Stewart became one of the world's wealthiest women.

After almost 30 years in town, however, she moved out. It was not long after she left Westport that she was convicted of insider trading. There was speculation that this would end her media empire. However, Martha is no wallflower, so after serving her sentence she came back as chairwoman and returned the company to profitability.

Cover by Perry Barlow

ROCK & ROLL HIGH SCHOOL

Don't let the dozing teachers behind this eager valedictorian give the impression that education is not taken seriously at Staples High School. The Westport Board of Education spends more than $100 million a year ensuring academic excellence throughout the entire school system.

But Staples also takes its entertainment seriously. From 1965 to 1969, the school's 1,200-seat theatre hosted an incredible series of rock stars—famous-name bands booked in by two students who loved the music that was the soundtrack to a sea change in American popular culture. The Animals, Cream, The Doors, the James Gang, Sly and the Family Stone, The Youngbloods, Taj Mahal and Richie Havens all played to admiring crowds in the Staples auditorium.

Just a few years before they morphed into Led Zeppelin, The Yardbirds made their American debut in front of a crowd at Staples. Also performing on center stage at Staples auditorium during this period were such classical musical luminaries as Leonard Bernstein on piano and Isaac Stern on violin, as well as Sammy Davis Jr. and Louis Armstrong.

Cover by Perry Barlow

OUT OF GAS

It was December, 1942 and America was at war in Europe and the Pacific. At home in Westport, young men were enlisting and everyone was saving rubber, glass, silk stockings—anything that could be reused in the war effort. Gasoline rationing was in effect across the entire country.

Garrett Price puts a happy face on the hardships of scarcity with this cover featuring a woman riding her bicycle away from Rippe's Farm Market in Westport with a Christmas tree resting on her handlebars.

Rippe's Farm Market on the Post Road was a family business: a retail farm stand with fruits, vegetables, annuals in spring, cider in the fall and Christmas trees and wreaths during the holidays. In 1977, the Rippe family sold the site to developers who built Harvest Commons, the first condos in town.

Cover by Garrett Price

COLD WAR ON NORTH AVENUE

This bucolic cover scene was published just as World War II was drawing to a close. The optimistic vision of fruit trees in bloom and manicured gardens belied the trouble that the Cold War would bring to Westport's doorstep.

In 1955, despite strong local opposition, the U.S. Army took possession of a site on North Avenue with plans to install a Nike anti-aircraft missile base. The numbers and types of missiles were classified information, but even the rumor of a military installation resulted in frenzied town meetings complete with protesters. However, plans proceeded and the site was built.

Technological developments eventually rendered the missiles obsolete and the Army decommissioned the site in 1963. Today, all traces have been removed from Westport's soil, but the Nike site turmoil inspired local writer Max Shulman to write the book *Rally Round the Flag, Boys*.

Cover by Edna Eicke

ARTISTIC BY NATURE

The determined artist on this cover is poised on his portable stool with his talent and his paintbrush, ready to replicate this lovely Westport dockside scene. Everything has been carefully arranged for maximum comfort and efficiency and all the elements of a perfect picture lie before him: sky, water, fishing boaaa... What happened to the boat?

Getting back to nature was one of the main reasons that many New York artists moved out of the city in the early 1900s. Open space, natural light and cheap rent made Westport an ideal location to establish an artists' colony. The move to Westport was dubbed the "art invasion" by a leading New York journal and the early presence of a few leading artists attracted more and more creative people to settle in town.

The list of artists who eventually made the town their home includes an incredible collection of illustrators who provided art and photographs for the great mass circulation magazines such as *The Saturday Evening Post, McCall's, Ladies' Home Journal, Good Housekeeping* and *Life*. And many of them were part of the Westport group that designed 167 U.S. postage stamps between 1958 and 1998.

Cover by Garrett Price

BURST OF ENERGY

Virtually no automobiles were produced in the United States in 1947, but the eastbound side of the Westport train station, where homecoming commuters disembark, was experiencing traffic jams. While the light is fading quickly, the resourceful woman on this cover has managed to find a spot to park her Nash Suburban woodie and is using a flashlight to help her husband spot her in the dark.

A trainload of commuters and a busy parking lot were just two signs of the postwar boom Westport experienced. The number of people living in Westport was roughly 10,000 leading up to the war. Ten years after, the number of residents had doubled. Imagine the extent of the construction activity, the challenges of educating a rapidly expanding school population and the difficulties of managing town budgets.

Today, the population of Westport stands at 26,000, and the railroad station parking lot, now well-lighted, still gets frantically crowded when the evening trains pull in on their way from New York City.

Cover by Garrett Price

The New Yorker

Oct. 4, 1947 — Price 20 cents

Garrett Price

THE LITTLE ENGINE THAT COULD

One hundred years before these children were drawn watching a freight train zoom by beneath a railroad bridge, Westport was battling to stop the "iron horse" from coming through town. The local gentry vehemently opposed the idea of noisy trains cutting across their farms, fouling the air, and frightening their livestock. They argued that the two-day stagecoach ride provided perfectly adequate access to New York City. The town lost the fight and in 1848 the railroad came to Westport. The town was paid $200 for the right-of-way, with the caveat that the tracks had to hug the shoreline so as not to disturb life in town.

Not only did Westport's town elders not recognize the value of a high-speed connection, but they gave away beautiful views of the salt marshes and Long Island Sound to the daily delight of train riders passing through on their way to New Haven or New York City.

In case you weren't aware, there's a small bridge over the Saugatuck River that's a hidden town treasure. At the end of Ferry Road you'll find a walking bridge that takes you across the river to the bustle of Saugatuck.

Cover by Edna Eicke

Oct. 9, 1948 — THE NEW YORKER — Price 20 cents

AND HERE'S THE STEEPLE

On this cover we see happy children spilling out of church, carrying presents on a Sunday morning before Christmas, while a handful of solemn adults enter quietly through a second entrance. The chapel, with its unusual square steeple and double entrance, belonged to Christ Episcopal Church, which was built at the northwest corner of the Post Road and Ludlow Street in Westport in 1835.

The image of the church was first captured in an 1835 engraving by the artist John Warner Barber and incorporated into Westport's official town seal. The building itself was torn down and replaced in 1884. In 1944, Christ Episcopal Church and the Memorial Church of the Holy Trinity merged to become Christ & Holy Trinity Church, located at the spot where in 1775 George Washington stopped for refreshments at what was then Disbrow Tavern.

Today, we are fortunate to have both the Westport town seal and this wonderful Edna Eicke illustration as a record of the unusual church and its square-shaped steeple.

Cover by Edna Eicke

Dec. 18, 1948 — **THE NEW YORKER** — Price 20 cents

SWEARING LIKE A SAILOR

Long Island Sound's steady winds attract serious sailors and casual boaters alike. As a community directly on the Sound, Westport has a strong maritime tradition dating as far back as the late 1700s, when boats left town with cargoes bound for New York, San Francisco and the Far East.

Ship captains such as Ned Wakeman, William Staples and the Sherwood triplets built houses on Saugatuck harbor so they could keep a watchful eye on their sailing ships. There was even a merchant ship building industry at Compo Cove.

Nowadays, Westport still is home to all manner of seafarers: The Cedar Point and Saugatuck Harbor Yacht Clubs cater to the topsider set; the boat basin at Compo Beach is equipped with more than 100 slips; and the Saugatuck River is home to a nationally ranked crew team as well as amateur paddleboarders.

Cover by Garrett Price

The New Yorker

July 9, 1949 — Price 20 cents

SCREEN TIME

When long-time resident Garrett Price illustrated this cover in 1950, Westport had not yet made its television debut, but since then it has had its fair share of small screen fame:

- Westport is where the Ricardos and the Mertzes moved when Lucy and Ricky left the city in the show *I Love Lucy*.

- Westport was the location of the first residence of Darrin and Samantha Stephens on the *Bewitched* series.

- *The Twilight Zone* had an episode called "A Stop at Willoughby," where the main character worked in New York City and commuted by train to his home in Westport. It aired on May 6, 1960, and the episode was written by then-Westport resident Rod Serling.

- In the series *The West Wing*, Bradley Whitford plays Josh Lyman, the White House deputy chief of staff, who comes from a Westport family.

- And, in the show *Boy Meets World*, Anthony Tyler Quinn plays Jonathan Turner, the main character's high school teacher, who is from Westport.

Cover by Garrett Price

THE NEW YORKER

April 29, 1950 · Price 20 cents

Garrett Price

WEST EGG?

This early-June cover depicts a couple and their dog as they arrive at their summer rental overlooking Compo Cove in Westport. While they must be happy to be out of the hustle and bustle of New York City they still face the task of emptying out their car and getting themselves installed.

Westport has a long history of attracting summer renters—none more famous than newlyweds F. Scott and Zelda Fitzgerald, who rented the Wakeman Cottage in the summer of 1920. The house was adjacent to what is now Longshore but was then a large, elegant estate complete with greenhouses, many uniformed servants and fancy cars. The Fitzgerald honeymoon summer in Westport was legendary for the wild parties they threw and for the literary figures who stayed with them for a night or two or three. F. Scott Fitzgerald wrote about this summer revelry in his second novel, *The Beautiful and Damned*.

A quote from the autobiography of artist Guy Pene du Bois, a fellow Westporter, sums up the scene: "In this Prohibition period the summers at Westport, Connecticut, exceeded the riotousness of New York. There gin and orange juice ruled the days and nights. Talk was an extravaganza. Work was an effort made between parties."

Cover by Garrett Price

June 3, 1950 · **THE NEW YORKER** · Price 20 cents

ON TRACK

The New York, New Haven and Hartford Railroad never did have the best record for on-time service, so this cover scene was a common one during the 1950s. Waiting patiently for the 6:24 train inside the Westport train station, wives, kids and even a dog (no men in sight) warm themselves around a pot-bellied stove, chatting and knitting while escaping from their unheated cars.

The commute from Westport to New York has changed quite a bit since then. Nowadays there are plenty of women who make the daily journey alongside their male colleagues. The train company's name also changed, to Conrail in 1969 and then to Metro-North in 1983. And, the daily peak round-trip fare that was under $3 in 1951 is now over $30.

Some things, however, have stayed the same, like the wood-panelled interior of the Westport train station and the bold NYNH&H logo printed on some old locomotives that still occasionally serve the commuter lines.

Cover by Perry Barlow

THE NEW YORKER

Mar. 3, 1951 — Price 20 cents

THE STAGE IS SET

The Westport Country Playhouse opened its doors in 1931 when New York theater producers Lawrence Langner and his wife, Armina Marshall, converted a tannery into a 500-seat theater. The stage was designed to make it easy to transfer successful productions directly to Broadway, and by the time this *New Yorker* cover appeared, several shows had already made the move from Westport to The Great White Way.

Staging productions in a cow barn that had been converted to a tannery before it became a theatre was challenging at times. When thunderstorms rolled in, the dialogue onstage could become so hard to hear that shows had to be suspended until the storms passed. And on one occasion, because of a power failure, people drove their cars up to the windows and pointed their headlights at the stage so that the show could go on.

Despite these early difficulties, the not-for-profit Playhouse has grown to become the area's premier theater. Nearly four million people have bought tickets. Seven hundred plays have been produced there, with thirty-six of them making it to Broadway. While the actors are all paid professionals, aspiring amateurs and interns—like Stephen Sondheim in his school years—can get in on the act.

Cover by Garrett Price

The New Yorker

June 2, 1951 — Price 20 cents

LIKE A TAG SALE

Tag sales, garage sales, yard sales and estate sales take place every weekend all over Westport. Some start early on Friday morning, a few are professionally run, and still others require you to take a ticket and wait for your turn before entering. For many shoppers, no retail experience is as gratifying as discovering the surprise bargain while rummaging through a jumble of stuff on your neighbor's front lawn.

The experience of living in Westport is similar to that of a tag sale. The residents are an eclectic mix, with different levels of wealth and influence— Connecticut Yankees, celebrities, immigrants, artists and corporate executives. The many ethnic groups, ages, professions and religions combine to make Westport a great place to call home.

Cover by Perry Barlow

The NEW YORKER

July 28, 1951 — Price 20 cents

GUARDING COMPO

Summer is over and the crowds have dispersed, so there is not much for this Westport lifeguard to watch out for. However, this was certainly not the case on April 25, 1777, when 26 warships carrying 1,800 British troops landed at Compo Beach. During the three-day incursion to destroy a munitions depot at Danbury, the Redcoats marched through town with only scattered opposition as they made their way to their destination 20 miles north.

After ransacking Danbury, torching homes and businesses and destroying military supplies stored there, the British troops started back to Compo Beach to reboard their warships. After a pitched battle at Ridgefield, the Redcoats were confronted in Westport by a hastily organized Minuteman militia. In the fighting that ensued, the Patriots battled fiercely right down to the beach as the Redcoats attempted to push their way back to their waiting ships.

In 1901, to commemorate this Revolutionary War battle, two cannons were placed at Compo Beach on the spot where the British came ashore. In 1910, the Minuteman statue, created by sculptor H. Daniel Webster, was erected facing Compo Hill, where the final battle took place. A complete restoration of the statue and its setting was completed in 2014.

Cover by Perry Barlow

Sept. 13, 1952 · THE NEW YORKER · Price 20 cents

HELLO MR. PRESIDENT

Greens Farms train station, the smaller of Westport's two, was built expressly for the convenience of railroad tycoon and local philanthropist Edward T. Bedford, to spare him from going all the way to Saugatuck from his Beachside Avenue mansion to board his private car. This cover depicts the tracks lined with people anxious to greet the next president one month before the 1952 election between Republican Dwight D. Eisenhower and Democrat Adlai Stevenson.

Many future presidents have stopped in Westport before becoming heads of state, starting with General George Washington, who took a break at Westport's Disbrow Tavern in 1775 on a horse ride to Boston. Candidate Abraham Lincoln was met in Bridgeport by a contingent of prominent Westporters in 1860 while rallying support for his antislavery platform. And, well-heeled Westporters welcomed Barack Obama at a fundraiser during his 2008 election campaign.

Cover by Perry Barlow

The New Yorker

Oct. 11, 1952 — Price 20 cents

CHANGING COLORS

The young girl on the tree swing on the cover is typical of most little kids in Westport: carefree, well-dressed and white. In fact, early attempts to make the schools in town more racially diverse met with strong opposition. When Westport's Board of Education proposed busing in fifty black Bridgeport students in the spring of 1970, a thousand people joined to hear the debate. Called Project Concern, it was an urban-suburban program sponsored by the state. Opponents lobbied fiercely for nine months and immediately after the board approved the plan in a 3-2 vote, a move for a recall election was begun to oust the chairwoman.

Despite appeals all the way to the state Supreme Court to block the vote, the decision was upheld and buses left Bridgeport each day for Burr Farms School, Coleytown and Bedford Elementary. Many local families rallied enthusiasically to help the Bridgeport students participate in all kinds of after-school activities. Host families arranged for ballet school, scouts, music lessons and Little League, and often served as overnight hosts. After ten years, however, the state ran out of funding for Project Concern, and attempts to find the money in the Westport School system also failed.

Cover by Edna Eicke

Oct. 18, 1952 — **THE NEW YORKER** — Price 20 Cents

HAPPY HOLIDAYS

On a cold December day, the kids excitedly approach the UPS truck parked on what could be one of the neighborhood streets close to Westport's downtown. The kids know that the brown boxes contain Christmas gifts, and since the cover appeared in 1953, Chanukah presents as well. Westport was a "restricted" community until World War II, with only a few well-known Jewish celebrities, plus a handful of other families—such as the Greenbergs, who owned a department store on Main Street—residing in town.

Things changed during the war, when several brokers split with the real estate board because of its word-of-mouth policy of not renting or selling to minorities. The dissidents opened the community up to anyone interested in moving in. Today, one in five Westport households is Jewish and there are two Jewish places of worship in town: Temple Israel, which opened its doors in 1959, and the Conservative Synagogue, founded in 1987.

Cover by Arthur Getz

The New Yorker

Dec. 19, 1953 — Price 20 cents

AHOY THERE

One hopes the bridgekeeper will hear the sailor's horn, fetch his long-handled socket wrench and open the Bridge Street Bridge to let this foursome through. Built in 1884 by the Union Bridge Company, the wrought-iron bridge spanning the Saugatuck River had a hand-cranked movable swing span. As it was the only surviving bridge of its type in Connecticut, it was listed on the National Register of Historic Places in 1987.

In the early 1990s, however, the state of Connecticut declared the bridge unsafe and proposed a wider span. But the neighbors' protests were heard in Hartford, and in the final design, the look of the bridge was preserved—although the hand crank was replaced by a motor.

In 2007, the bridge was dedicated in memory of William F. Cribari, a firefighter and World War II veteran, known to many commuters as the man who creatively directed traffic in Saugatuck through winter storms and summer heat.

Cover by Garrett Price

Aug. 7, 1954 — The NEW YORKER — Price 20 cents

DAYBREAK

For seventy years, when you exited the Merritt Parkway in Westport, you drove past the handsome greenhouse at Daybreak Nursery. Evan Harding acquired the greenhouse structure from a Greenwich estate and opened the business on the day that Pearl Harbor was attacked in 1941.

In addition to selling flowers, plants and trees, Harding was a landscape designer who served on Westport's Planning and Zoning Commission for many years. It was Harding who championed the idea of using the excess material generated by the construction of I-95 to fill in the Saugatuck River behind Main Street to make more parking.

The Parker Harding Plaza (sometimes referred to jokingly as Harder Parking Plaza) bears his name along with that of town Selectman Emerson Parker. Unfortunately, the greenhouse that inspired this cover is no longer standing, having been largely destroyed by fire in 2013.

Cover by Edna Eicke

The New Yorker

May 7, 1955

Price 20 cents

McMANSION

This charming house is the Dolan House at the corner of Bridge Street and Imperial Avenue in Westport. Mr. Dolan tended the nearby swing bridge, and this cover might depict his granddaughter sitting on the front steps waiting to celebrate the 4th of July. The house was built in 1875, and what makes it special is that it is still around and still looks just as it always did from Bridge Street, though it has been expanded over the years with additions and renovations.

Westporters are so comfortable with changing and rebuilding houses that "Teardown of the Day" is a feature on our local website. One builder may be demolishing a home while right next door another contractor may be restoring an antique. McMansions are replacing split-levels and capes all over town.

Nonetheless, the Westport Historical Society has identified close to 350 houses in town, like the Dolan House, that were built over 100 years ago and still are standing proudly today.

Cover by Edna Eicke

The New Yorker

June 30, 1956

Price 20 cents

Edna Eicke

ABSTRACT HOLIDAY

After a summer vacation spent by the shore, you would expect this artist to return home with lovingly painted boats, lighthouses and fishermen to conjure up the sights, sounds and smells of the seaside. Instead, the car is filled with canvas after canvas covered with abstract shapes, forms, colors and textures. Where are the boats? Where are the buoys?

Maybe the young lady on this cover should have enrolled for classes with Westport's Famous Artists School. Opened in 1947 on Wilton Road across the river from downtown, the correspondence school boasted a world-class faculty that included Norman Rockwell. Students of all ages applied by filling in "Draw Me" magazine ads. At its peak, the school had more than 40,000 students.

Sadly, overexpansion, bad business decisions and the death of founder Albert Dorne eventually forced bankruptcy. Even so, Famous Artists School had a lasting impact on our town, both for the many talented local artists it brought here and because it helped establish an international reputation for Westport as a community that embraced creativity.

Cover by Arthur Getz

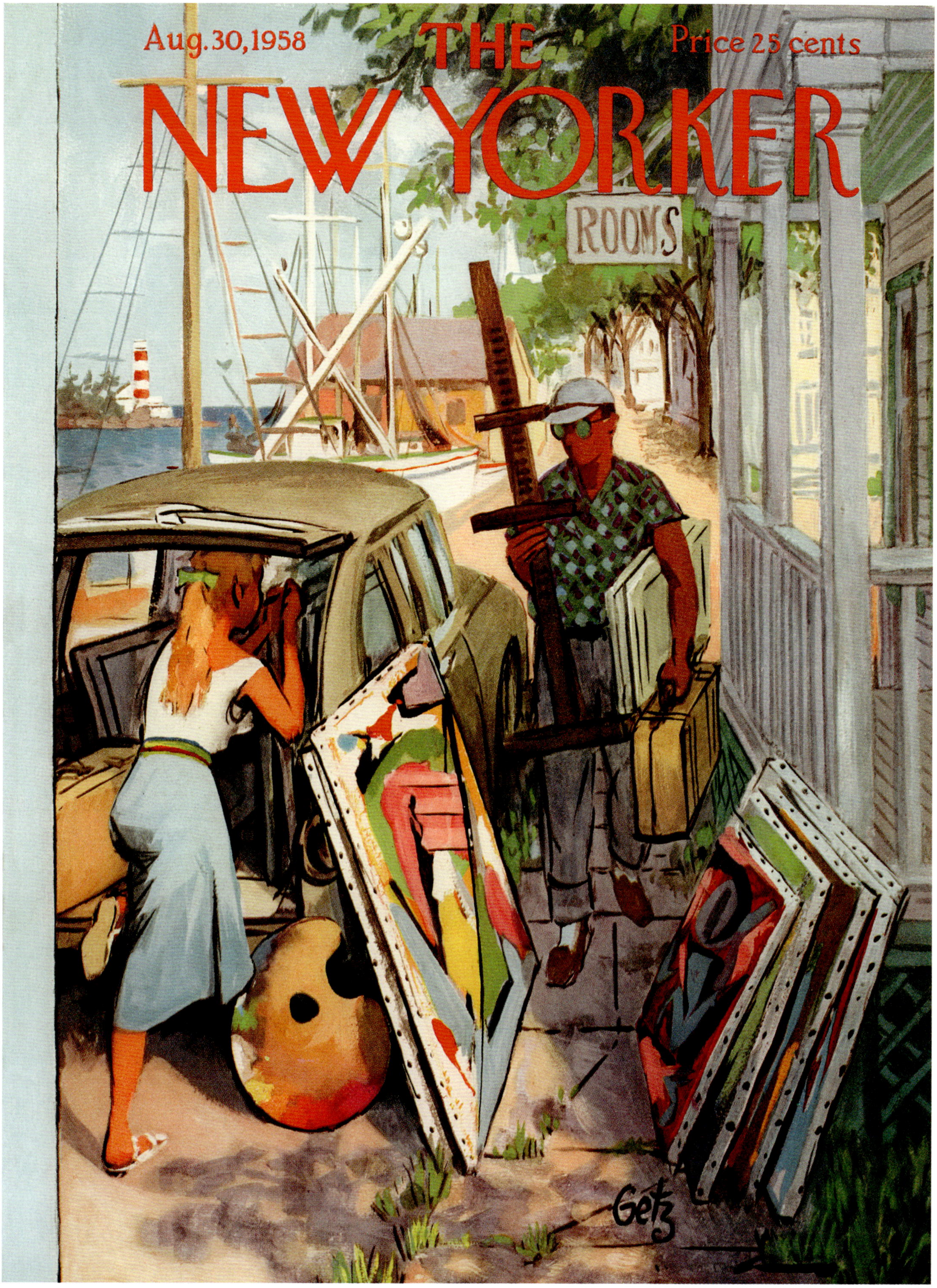
Aug. 30, 1958
THE
NEW YORKER
Price 25 cents
ROOMS
Getz

ALL-AMERICAN CITY

As the summer of 1958 was winding down and fall's foliage was presenting itself in its full glory as pictured on this *New Yorker* cover, Westport was about to be honored as an "All-American City," one of ten communities in the country recognized by the National Civic League annually for tackling community-wide challenges and achieving uncommon results.

The national award was based on six areas of competition: government structure, rational land use, tax reform, education, refuse disposal and a sound police organization. Westport was flooded with posters, bumper stickers and flags—all celebrating the coveted honor.

Town officials accepted kudos from President Dwight D. Eisenhower, Connecticut Senator Thomas Dodd and Governor Abraham Ribicoff. The award, which has been called "The Nobel Prize" for constructive citizenship, put Westport on the map as a town that was in the forefront of American civic achievement.

Cover by Arthur Getz

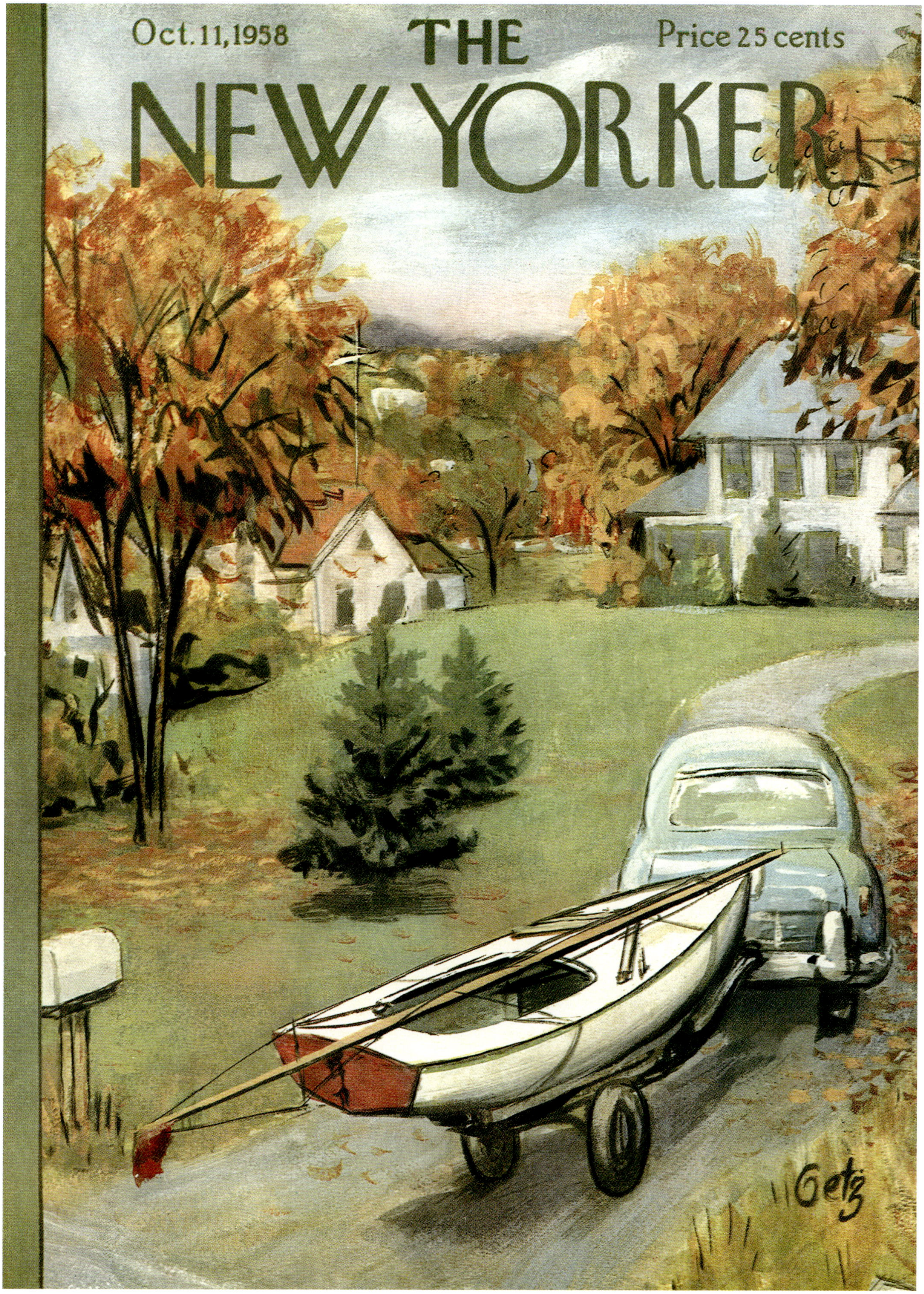
Oct. 11, 1958
THE
NEW YORKER
Price 25 cents
Getz

ROUND POND

This *New Yorker* cover is reminiscent of Round Pond on Compo Road South, where skaters can often be seen gliding on the winter ice. In addition to its natural beauty, the pond is historically significant for having been owned by Lillian Wald, one of the most influential and respected social reformers of the 20th century. She lived in the "House on the Pond" until she passed away in 1940.

Legend has it that she was related to the King of Poland, but it was the social reforms that she championed in the poverty-stricken Lower East Side of Manhattan that earned this champion of women, children and the downtrodden a place in New York University's Hall of Fame for Great Americans.

Her life-long engagement in social issues led to lasting friendships with thousands of people, some poor and obscure, and some rich and famous. Among the notables who signed the guestbook at her home in Westport were President and Mrs. Franklin D. Roosevelt, New York Mayor Fiorello La Guardia, Cardinal Hayes, Chief Justice Charles Evans Hughes and Albert Einstein.

Cover by Edna Eicke

The New Yorker

Feb. 28, 1959 — Price 25 cents

Edna Eicke

ADVICE FROM THE GRAVE

Since this *New Yorker* cover was published, professional golf has become a sport with multimillion-dollar purses and global sponsorships, but for a duffer like the one pictured here, not much has changed. Golfers, then and now, often find their errant golf balls—if they find them at all—in quite unusual places. In this case, he has discovered his ball in Gray's Cemetery off the 13th fairway at the Longshore golf course in Westport.

Although now a premier 18-hole course with a majestic tree-lined entrance, well-bunkered greens and views of Long Island Sound, in the 1700s Longshore was an onion farm that included a small cemetery that was the final resting place of Henry Gray, one of Westport's founders. In the early 1900s, the farm became an estate for an oil baron who sold it to a group that converted it into a private country club. In 1960, however, the club ran into financial trouble, and after many heated debates about whether it was a wise use of public funds, Westport acquired the 169-acre property for just $1.9 million and turned it into a public country club open to all Westport citizens.

Cover by Whitney Darrow, Jr.

Aug. 22, 1959
THE NEW YORKER
Price 25 cents
SPENT NOT
HIS LIFE
IN
IDLE PLAY
Whitney Darrow, jr

ART ABOUT TOWN

This cover depicts the very popular outdoor art show that takes place on Main Street in Westport every summer. After a season on the shore, it's not surprising that we find lots of boats and lighthouses. Many of these paintings will end up above someone's living room fireplace, while a few might have the good fortune of becoming part of the town's very own public art collection.

The first public art in Westport was commissioned by President Roosevelt's Works Progress Administration in the 1930s, when a distinguished group of Westport artists created art for the town's public buildings. In 1964, Bert Chernow, an artist and teacher who recognized the importance of art in the daily lives of schoolchildren, founded the Westport Schools Permanent Art Collection.

Today, the town's collection consists of more than 1,800 original pieces by world-famous artists such as Picasso, Calder and Motherwell, as well as hundreds of works by Westport artists such as George Hand Wright, Stevan Dohanos, Howard Munce and Leonard Everett Fisher. All art in the collection was donated and, thanks to a dedicated volunteer committee, rotates on display through the town's schools and public buildings, a testament to Westport's continuing dedication and reverence for artists and what they produce.

Cover by Garrett Price

Aug. 29, 1959
THE NEW YORKER
Price 25 cents
OUTDOOR ART FESTIVAL
BANK
NEW YORK
NEW LONDON
GROTON
AIRPORT
PAINT STORE
FURN
Garrett Price

MY WAY OR THE HIGHWAY

A truly national transportation system was the goal of President Eisenhower in the 1950s, and plans were put in place for a new interstate highway to run through Connecticut. Governor John Davis Lodge, himself a Westporter, was unswerving in his support for the truck route to ease the snarled traffic and screeching truck brakes that were all too common on the two-lane Post Road.

Dozens of homes and businesses, and even the Saugatuck Methodist Church, were demolished to make way for the new turnpike. This cover shows a steam shovel and bulldozers cutting a swath alongside Greens Farms Road in Westport.

Local legend maintains that disenchantment with the disruption of the highway construction led to Lodge's 1954 gubernatorial defeat at the hands of Democrat Abe Ribicoff who, for a time, was also a Westport resident. Ironically, I-95 is now officially known as the Governor John Davis Lodge Turnpike.

Cover by Arthur Getz

May 21, 1960 — The NEW YORKER — Price 25 cents

THE FUNNIES

What better way to spend a summer morning than sprawled out on the lawn catching up on the antics of your favorite characters from the weekly comics drawn by one of Westport's many accomplished cartoonists. Among the most well-known were:

Dick Browne (Hagar the Horrible)
Mel Casson (Sparky)
Stan Drake (Blondie)
Hank Ketchum (Dennis the Menace)
Bud Sagendorf (Popeye)
Leonard Starr (Annie)
Curt Swan (Superman)
Mort Walker (Beetle Bailey)

They were all part of a close-knit group of cartoonists who had rollicking weekly get-togethers to discuss their witty commentaries on the foibles of the human condition at Mario's Restaurant, across from the Saugatuck train station. Creating funny cartoons every day is hard work and this group knew how to get away for a few hours each week to gain some relief from their solitary drawing board tasks.

Cover by Edna Eicke

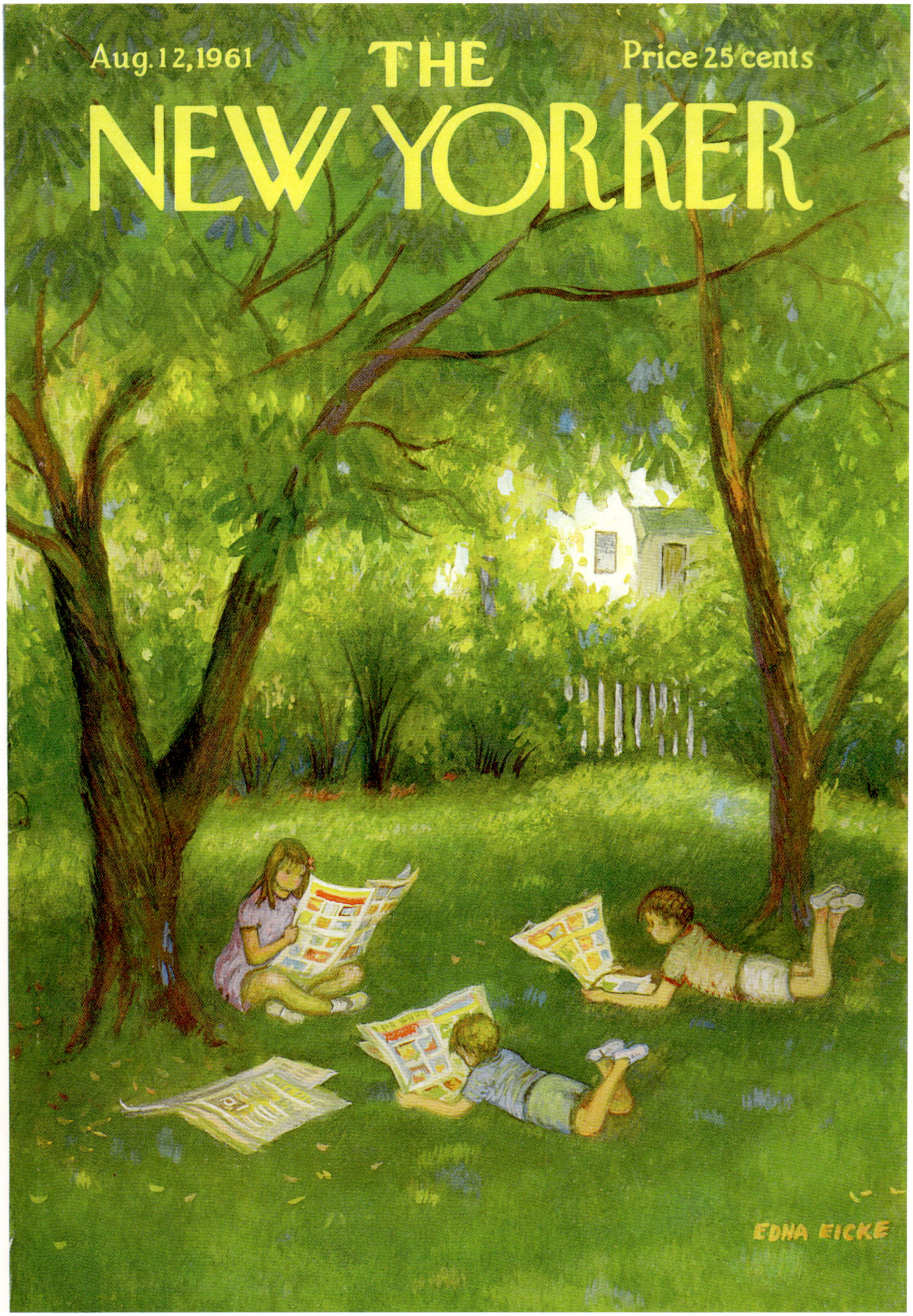
Aug. 12, 1961
THE
NEW YORKER
Price 25 cents
EDNA EICKE

PARTING IS SUCH SWEET SORROW

There is a sense of melancholy in this cover as friends say goodbye at the Westport train station after a Labor Day weekend together. They are tired and sunburned after a picnic at Compo Beach, a stroll down Main Street and an open-air concert at the Levitt.

The Levitt Pavilion for the Performing Arts, providing free programs thanks in part to the support of residents Mimi and Mortimer Levitt, was built on the site of the old town dump. To prove that the site was sanitary, Amy Vanderbilt, the American authority on etiquette at the time, held a white-gloved, lifted-pinky tea party atop the closed landfill.

Since the Levitt opened, over one million guests have been entertained by acts such as Ray Charles, Tom Jones, Don McLean, Smokey Robinson, Roberta Flack, Frankie Valli, Willie Nelson, Count Basie, Judy Collins, Foreigner and The Doobie Brothers, as well as resident stars like Michael Bolton, Ashford & Simpson, Meatloaf, Corky Laing and Neil Sedaka.

Cover by Arthur Getz

THE NEW YORKER

Sept. 1, 1962 — Price 25 cents

HOW 'BOUT THEM APPLES?

A favorite journey back in time for Westporters is a trip to Aspetuck Orchards in neighboring Easton. Little has changed since this illustration was a *New Yorker* cover. Today, as then, the red buildings are bursting with baskets full of an astonishing selection of apple varieties along with shelves laden with pies, jams, and cider.

Westport's own orchards have long since disappeared, but evidence of our farming past still exists around town: Greens Farms was named after John Green, the largest of the original landholders who colonized Westport in 1648. Nyala Farms was a 52-acre Guernsey cow dairy farm named by Edward T. Bedford's son after seeing the nyala, a spiral-horned antelope, while on an African safari. And the Wakeman Farms Athletic Fields were the site of a 38-acre farm that operated until 1970.

So the next time you are going down Adams Farm Road, Burr Farms Road, Flower Farm Road, Gray's Farm Road, Hedley Farms Road or Sherwood Farms Lane, remember that you are traveling through a part of Westport's rural past.

Cover by Garrett Price

Nov. 10, 1962
THE NEW YORKER
Price 25 cents
ASPETUCK ORCHARDS
CIDER
Garrett Price

DOWN BY THE RIVER

This serene cover image of Saugatuck harbor with its steel railroad bridge, boats and buildings bathed in blue, makes it easy to forget the neighborhood's early history. In the 1700s, Saugatuck bustled with shippers, merchants and manufacturers. The spirit of free enterprise along the river led to the construction of numerous small factories and workshops that produced a variety of products and catered to the shipping trade, including manufacturers of ivory buttons and coffin tacks.

At that time, there was no Westport; the Saugatuck River was the dividing line between Fairfield and Norwalk. In 1835, Saugatuck, the downtown and Greens Farms areas were incorporated into the single town of Westport. The building of the railroad in 1848 brought immigrants from Ireland and Italy. The Catholic Church of the Assumption was established to fill the religious needs of the new arrivals and the Sons of Italy became the heart of the community.

All these many years later, Saugatuck still retains its unpretentious roots; just ask anyone who has spent a late night on the half sunken Black Duck barge tavern, whose motto is: "Lose your liver down by the river."

Cover by Arthur Getz

Nov. 30, 1963 · The NEW YORKER · Price 25 cents

HIGHWAY FIT FOR A KING

This winter scene is set where Riverside Avenue meets the Post Road before you get to the bridge to downtown Westport. Happily, some of the buildings shown on this 1965 cover are still standing today, but the most enduring element has been the road itself.

What became the Post Road was built at the direction of Charles II, King of England, so that mail could be delivered safely between New York and Boston. Trees and brush were cleared from along an existing Pequot Indian trail that traversed Connecticut. On January 22, 1673, the first rider set out on the two-week journey delivering mail to Boston. Benjamin Franklin, in his role as one of two U.S. deputy postmasters for British North America, suggested improvements to the King's Highway in 1753, adding a small bridge across the Saugatuck River. Later he personally supervised the placing of milestone markers along the Post Road as a means of setting accurate postal rates.

The Post Road grew to become a prime commercial thoroughfare. Efforts to broaden Westport's tax base in the 1970s brought a relaxing of building regulations and consequently a marked increase in business construction. Most evident, and most controversial, was the large Wright Street building that looms on the hill just behind the small buildings that still stand at the corner.

Cover by Albert Hubbell

Jan. 9, 1965
THE
NEW YORKER
Price 25 cents
VILLAGE MARKET
Albert Hubbell

MAY FLOWERS

In Westport, many people feel that late spring is the most beautiful time of the year. Following long winters and rainy Aprils, May finally bursts onto the scene bringing such wonders as leafy trees, brightly colored azaleas and sweet smelling flowers. Of course, it is not yet summer and not yet time for that well-deserved vacation; one is still commuting to work each morning.

Pictured here is the train station with a gaggle of commuters awaiting the arrival of the train that will take them to the "City." Some people are reading their morning papers, others chatting, but one character prefers to be alone; a businessman with his paper under his arm and briefcase in hand, striding forward carrying a large bunch of lilacs. He is on his way to work, but what's the story? When he arose that morning, was he so moved by the lilacs that he wanted to transfer the beauty of his garden to his office? Or is he bringing the flowers for someone else? We don't know, but it's a delightful speculation.

Cover by Charles Saxon

May 1, 1965 — The NEW YORKER — Price 25 cents

KNOW YOUR ONIONS

There were a number of thriving hardware stores on Westport's Main Street when this cover was published. Welch's Hardware store was one of them, Hartman's Hardware was another, and Westport Hardware opened a bit later. During spring season each year, in addition to the usual lawn tools, these hardware stores sold onion sets: little seedlings in bare-root bundles that were a throwback to the Civil War days when Westport was a national center for onion growing.

The high vitamin C content of onions helped to ward off scurvy, so pickled onions were added to field rations, and battlefield hospitals used pickled onion juice to heal wounds and prevent gangrene. During the Civil War, Westport was the largest provider of onions to the Union Army, with seventy-five local farms involved in the industry. Demand for onions grown in town continued to be strong until a cutworm plague wiped out the crop in the early 1900s.

This, however, does not mean that onions stopped growing in Westport altogether. The first local sign of spring is when the air is permeated with the pungent odor of wild onion grass—a reminder of those long-ago onions.

Cover by Arthur Getz

May 7, 1966

The NEW YORKER

Price 35 cents

PEACE & QUIET

Arthur Getz was in the process of moving from New York City to Connecticut when this appeared as a *New Yorker* cover. If what is pictured here is any indication, the artist is clearly looking forward to a quieter and more bucolic life than he was experiencing in a city roiled at the time by anti-Vietnam war protests and a student revolt that brought Columbia University to its knees.

The library he has drawn is an island of calm shielded from life's menacing storms and troubled times, a place of quiet contemplation, a place to read and to think. For a long time after its founding in 1886, the Westport Public Library was just such a place. Growing and evolving with the times, however, the library has become a community center and even boasts a "Maker Space" where visitors come to use 3D printers and construct robots and toy trucks.

Cover by Arthur Getz

June 29, 1968

THE NEW YORKER

Price 35 cents

BRIGHT LIGHTS, SMALL TOWN

Connecticut winters can be long and cold, but the bright lights still beckon. This was especially true at the intersection of the Post Road and Cedar Road, where on one side you had The Cedar Brook Cafe and on the other Krazy Vins. In the early years, patrons of the Brook were referred to as "artistic." But by the 1970s, when gay people came out more publicly, this was the center of gay life in Fairfield County. Krazy Vins was a strip club popular for its topless female dancers. Who knew?

After closing time, customers from both bars could be found just two doors down at the Sherwood Diner enjoying a snack. The Cedar Brook Cafe closed in 2010, giving up its claim as the oldest continually operating gay bar in America. Krazy Vins moved out a number of years earlier and was replaced by a Starbucks. Meanwhile, the Sherwood Diner is still open 24 hours a day, 7 days a week and warmly welcomes early risers as well as night owls.

Cover by David Preston

Jan. 25, 1969 **THE** Price 50 cents
NEW YORKER

THE GRIT IN THE OYSTER

In 1890, Captain Walter Allen built a restaurant on the edge of Westport's Mill Pond that was the inspiration for this cover. Allen's Clam House served freshly caught seafood, and its specialty was the clams and oysters harvested right outside its back door. After serving meals to locals and out-of-towners alike for over a century, the sagging building with its slanting floors proved too tough to renovate. So the town bought the property in 1999 and turned the site into a nature preserve.

Today, neither clams nor oysters are commercially fished out of the Mill Pond, but there are plenty in the deeper waters of Long Island Sound. A handful of companies, mostly owned and operated by military veterans, harvest and sell oysters. Famed for their juicy meats, robust taste, and deeply cupped shells, Bluepoint, Saddle Rock and Great White oysters found off the coast of Westport are shipped to restaurants around the world.

Cover by Albert Hubbell

Aug. 16, 1969

The NEW YORKER

Price 50 cents

SHERWOOD ISLAND WAR

This cover could depict any summer weekend at Sherwood Island State Park, with everyone relaxing under their umbrellas while the lifeguard does his best, sporting a shirt with a matching pattern. This halcyon beach scene, however, belies the turmoil that went into creating Connecticut's first public-access beach.

It was dubbed the "23-year war," and it was fought between the State Parks Commission and a group of large Greens Farms landowners. The State was determined to find a shorefront park in Fairfield County that would be open to the public. The chosen land at the time had many owners and a few powerful developers who wanted to convert the 234-acre former Sherwood farm into a densely packed housing development.

In 1937, the Parks Commission finally prevailed, thanks to the support of civic-minded Westporters who believed in preserving open space for the benefit of all.

Cover by Charles Saxon

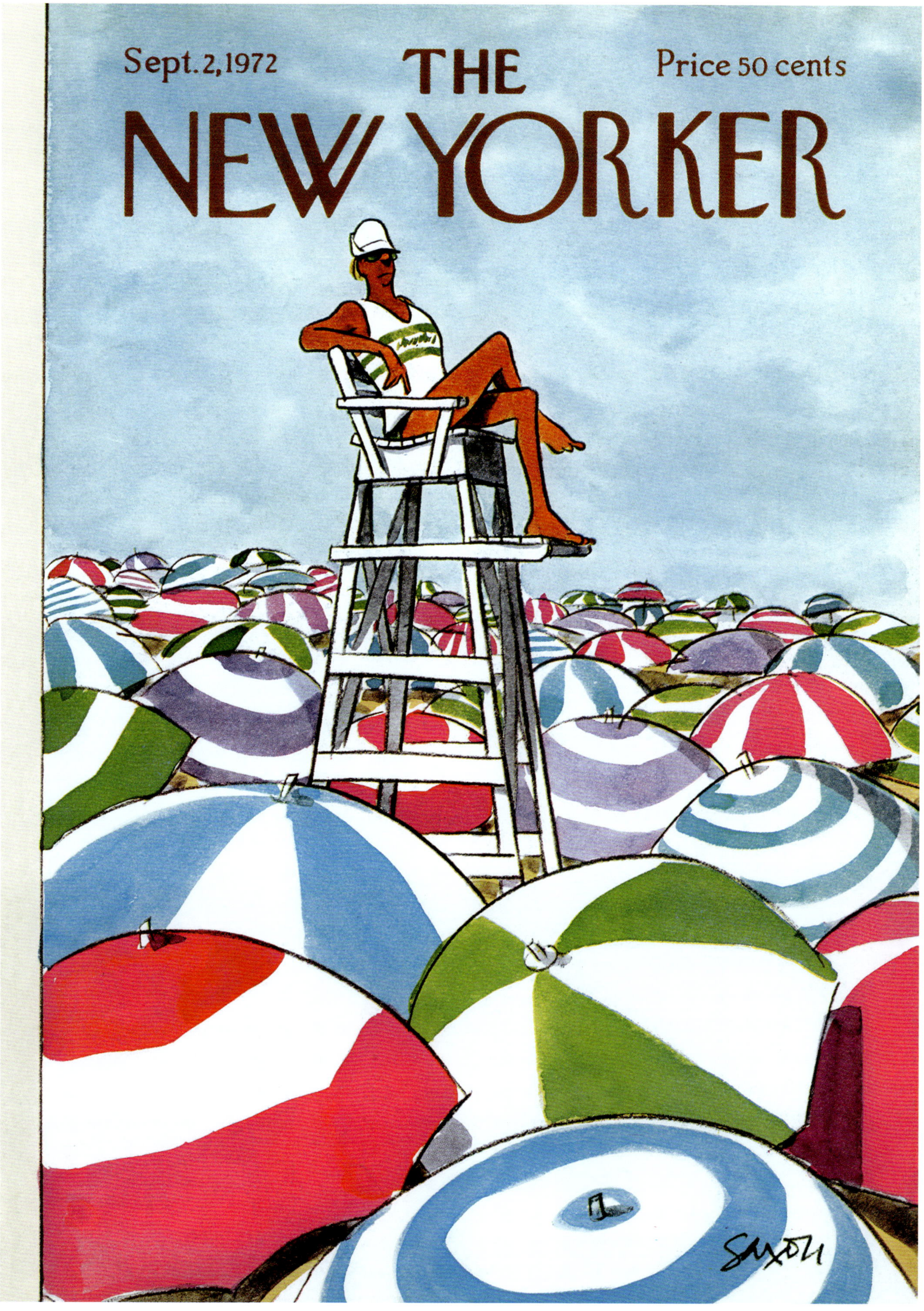
Sept. 2, 1972
THE
NEW YORKER
Price 50 cents
Saxon

ATOMIC PLANT OFF COMPO

The most iconic image of Westport is the pavilion at Compo Beach as captured on this *New Yorker* cover on a summer day. Originally named "Compaug," which meant "the bears' fishing ground" in Native American language, the beach is a wonderful place to sit and look out across the open waters of Long Island Sound.

But this pristine view was almost destroyed in 1967, when the United Illuminating Company of Bridgeport announced plans to build a 14-story nuclear power plant on Cockenoe Island, a 28-acre island vegetated by wild roses and sea lavender and populated by herons, egrets and plovers just a mile off Compo Beach.

For two years, citizens of Westport battled against the plan in town hall meetings and with Save Cockenoe Now rallies and posters. Finally, enough pressure was brought to bear that the utility company was forced to cancel its plans, and the island was sold to the town for $200,000.

Cover by Albert Hubbell

The New Yorker

Aug. 20, 1973

Price 50 cents

SORRY, WE'RE CLOSED

Today, Main Street in downtown Westport is lined with some of the nation's best-known boutiques and luxury store brands. But ask any Westporter and you will find that no matter how young or old, there is a bygone shop that they miss. The long list of downtown stores that are no longer open for business includes:

Barneys	Klein's
Barnum Travel	Linen Closet
Ben Franklin	Max's Art Supplies
Bill's Smoke Shop	Melody House Music
Charles Food Shop	Oakes Automotive Service
Country Bazaar	Pickwick Gift Shop
Country Gal	Rico Beauty Salon
Dorain's Drugs	Shilepsky's Clothing
Dress Box	The Remarkable Bookstore
Economy Liquors	Town & Country Shoes
Greenberg's Dept. Store	Townley Restaurant
Gristede Brothers Grocers	Tracy's Menswear
Hartman's Hardware	Swerdling's Bakery
Henry Lehr	Westlake Restaurant
Isabel Eland Shop	Westport Food Center

Not to mention the "hardware-gifts-souvenirs-novelties" shop pictured on this cover.

Cover by Albert Hubbell

The New Yorker

July 8, 1974 — Price 50 cents

ROLLING CHURCH

Playing host to an event under the tent, the Saugatuck Congregational Church looks so perfect on this cover that you'd never guess it wasn't always in the location where you see it today: on the north side of the Post Road above the corner of Myrtle Avenue.

The church originally stood on the south side of the Post Road near Compo Road. But on August 28, 1951, the 200-ton building was moved 600 feet diagonally across the street using giant logs as rollers as thousands of Westporters watched in awe. The task took ten hours to complete and became a national story when pictures of Westport's rolling church appeared in *Life* magazine.

After more than 60 years of peaceful worship, the congregation was once again on the move just before Thanksgiving, 2011—but this time it was due to a fire that severely damaged the church. During the three-year reconstruction project, Congregational services were held at Temple Israel, providing another fine example of Westport's ecumenical nature.

Cover by Arthur Getz

Sept. 8, 1986 — **THE NEW YORKER** — Price $1.50

LEND ME A HAND

Charles Addams, creator of the Addams Family, was the most famous *New Yorker* cartoonist of his generation. With a reputation as a ladies' man, he is said to have had girlfriends throughout Fairfield County. Though it is impossible to pinpoint exactly where the idea for this cover came from, perhaps it was during a round of golf at Longshore in Westport.

In his illustration, Addams draws upon Arthurian legend as a way of suggesting the magic, at least for a golfer, of being able to hit a ball that had previously found its way into a water hazard. Not only is this golfer able to strike the ball, but it has been raised to perfect height by none other than The Lady of the Lake, known best for providing King Arthur with Excalibur.

Does this impress our golfer? Not in the least. Reflecting Addams' strange and slightly twisted sense of humor, there is no expression of surprise or awe on his face; no, he has merely taken his stance in preparation for hitting his next shot without seeming to take notice of his "caddy's" extraordinary powers.

Cover by Charles Addams

May 23, 1988

THE NEW YORKER

Price $1.75

ABOUT THE ARTISTS

CHARLES ADDAMS (1912~1988)

"Chas" Addams grew up in Westfield, New Jersey, and attended Colgate University before graduating from the University of Pennsylvania. Later he studied at the Grand Central School of Art in New York City. He was a prolific cartoonist for *The New Yorker*. The darkly humorous and macabre characters he developed became so popular that they took on a life of their own as The Addams Family of TV and movie fame. Although he never owned a home in Westport, he was a popular Westport guest and spent many weekends at different addresses around town.

PERRY BARLOW (1892~1977)

Perry Barlow was raised in Texas and attended the School of the Art Institute of Chicago. After graduation, he wound up in New York City, where he met and fell in love with fellow Art Institute graduate Dorothy Hope Smith. They were married in 1922 and shortly thereafter moved to Westport. Barlow produced 135 covers for *The New Yorker* in addition to thousands of cartoons. His work featured a loose, sketchy style. He is considered one of *The New Yorker's* most prolific artists. Because he was color blind, the soft watercolors in his paintings were often applied by his wife—the creator of the drawing of the baby on the Gerber Baby Food label.

WHITNEY DARROW, JR. (1909~1999)

Whitney Darrow Jr. went to Princeton University and moved to New York after graduation. He was torn between becoming either a lawyer or a cartoonist. In the end, the fact that *The New Yorker's* offices were only a few blocks from his apartment decided his career. He returned to live in Connecticut at the start of World War II, moving to nearby Wilton and helping out at the Westport-Weston Chapter of the Red Cross. Although he is credited with only two *New Yorker* covers, his skill at capturing middle-class suburban lifestyles was seen in more than 1,500 cartoons in *The New Yorker* from 1933 until his retirement in 1982. He was considered a master draftsman and a witty, satiric cartoonist who, unlike some of his colleagues, also wrote his own captions.

JAMES DAUGHERTY (1889~1974)

For more than 50 years, James Daugherty, born in Asheville, North Carolina, lived, worked and raised his family in Westport. He was an active member of the community and a founding member of the Westport-Weston Arts Council. Renowned for his drawing skills, two of his stylized "sport" illustrations became *New Yorker* covers in the first years of the magazine's existence. Throughout his career, Daugherty, who often signed himself as "Jimmy the Ink," used pure color to create powerful works of art. Several of his paintings are in the collections at both MOMA and the Whitney Museum of American Art.

EDNA EICKE (1919~1979)

Edna Eicke was born in Montclair, New Jersey, and attended Parsons School of Design in New York. In 1953 she moved with her husband, the artist Tom Funk, and their three children to Westport, Connecticut. She had a clean, precise, almost primitive style, with an air of sophistication. Her images were beautifully composed and carefully crafted. She was responsible for 51 *New Yorker* covers that often depicted local Westport scenes and often featured her children.

ARTHUR GETZ (1913~1996)

Born in Passaic, New Jersey, in 1913, Arthur Getz was such a natural talent that he earned a full scholarship to Pratt Institute in Brooklyn. Getz moved to New York City in 1935 and immediately sold drawings to *The New Yorker*, where his association spanned more than 50 years. Getz spent many summers in the Old Mill Beach area and later moved to Sharon, Connecticut. He had a superb eye for composition, color and the effects of light. Getz earned the honor of being the most published *New Yorker* cover artist of all time, with 213 covers to his name.

ALICE HARVEY (1894~1983)

Born in Chicago, Alice Harvey attended the Art Institute of Chicago and then the Arts Students League in New York. When *The New Yorker* was launched, she was one of the first illustrators brought on board. Many of her cartoons and two of her covers were published. In the 1920s she moved to Westport from New York with her husband Charles Ramsey, and they lived in town for the rest of their lives. Her daughter, Janet, still lives in Westport, and remembers her mother's warm friendships with the other *New Yorker* artists who followed her lead and became her neighbors.

HELEN HOKINSON (1893~1949)

Helen was born in Mendota, Illinois, and studied art at the Academy of Fine Arts in Chicago and then at Parsons School of Design in New York. Shortly after *The New Yorker* came into being, she submitted a drawing and it was accepted. Plump, upper-class dowagers wearing dresses, hats and high-heeled shoes and often sporting an attendant butler were the hallmarks of "Hokinson women." In addition to 68 covers, more than 1,500 of her cartoons appeared in *The New Yorker*. After she established herself professionally in New York, she moved to Wilton and became a member of the Westport Women's Club. Sadly, her life was cut short when her plane crashed flying to Washington to receive an award.

ALBERT HUBBELL (1908~1994)

Albert Hubbell's realist *New Yorker* covers often featured Westport scenes. He came from Duluth, Minnesota, to study at the Art Student's League in New York before spending time studying in Paris. He worked at *The New Yorker* for many years, contributing not only art but commentary and fiction. Hubbell produced 19 covers for *The New Yorker* and was the magazine's temporary art director for a brief stint in 1943, filling in while James Geraghty was participating in classes for the Volunteer Officer Corps. He married the sister of another *New Yorker* cartoonist, Dana Fradon, and moved to Westport.

DAVID PRESTON (1916~1984)

David Preston spent his early childhood in Scarsdale, but the family soon moved to Weston where they lived for 50 years. In 1935, he started college at Cornell, later transferring to MIT. Preston considered himself a science writer-reporter rather than an illustrator; nevertheless, three of his drawings made it onto the covers of *The New Yorker*. In the 1960s he lived on Washington Street in Westport with his second wife, Jessie, the assistant director of the Public Library.

GARRETT PRICE (1897~1979)

Garrett Price was born in Bucyrus, Kansas, and attended the University of Wyoming and the Art Institute of Chicago. He was an early contributor to *The New Yorker*, and drew 99 covers and numerous cartoons. He moved to his home on Canal Street in Westport in the 1930s and continued to live there and provide *The New Yorker* with illustrations into his eighties. When he retired, he was pensioned for life in recognition of having been one of the founding members of *The New Yorker*, working there from 1925 until 1974.

CHARLES SAXON (1920~1988)

Born in Brooklyn, Charles Saxon graduated from Columbia University in 1940. He served as a bomber pilot during World War II and began drawing cartoons on weekends. In 1956, he became a staff cartoonist at *The New Yorker* and was a close friend of art editor James Geraghty, spending many hours socializing and traveling with the Geraghtys. When he married his wife, Nancy, the couple moved to Silvermine and then to New Canaan, where they lived for 34 years. Charles Saxon's elegant drawings satirize the lifestyles of his sophisticated neighbors in Westport and other Fairfield County towns. He is credited with 92 *New Yorker* covers and more than 700 cartoons.

INDEX

Actors, 14
Addams, Charles, 106, 108
All-American City award, 68
Allen's Clam House, 96
Aspetuck Orchards, 82
Barber, John Warner, 38
Barlow, Perry, 16, 20, 22, 24, 26, 46, 50, 52, 54, 108
Baron's property, 10
Bedford, Edward T., 10, 54, 82
Bolton, Michael, 80
Black Duck, 84
Bridge Street bridge, 60
Cartoonists, 78
Cedar Brook Café, 94
Charles Food Shop, 16
Chernow, Bert, 74
Christ and Holy Trinity Church, 38
Christ Episcopal Church, 38
Civil War, 90
Cockenoe Island, 100
Compo Beach battle, 52
Compo House, 10
Compo Pavilion, 100
Conservative Synagogue, 58
Cribari, William F., 60
Darrow, Whitney, Jr., 72, 108
Daugherty, James, 8, 108
Daybreak Nursery, 62
Disbrow Tavern, 38, 54
Dolan House, 64
Dorne, Albert, 66
Eicke, Edna, 30, 36, 38, 56, 62, 64, 70, 78, 108
Einstein, Albert, 70
Eisenhower, Dwight D., 54, 68, 76
Evyan perfume, 10
Famous Artists School, 66
Fitzgerald, F. Scott and Zelda, 44
Franklin, Benjamin, 86
Getz, Arthur, 58, 66, 68, 76, 80, 84, 90, 92, 104, 108
Great Depression 12, 20, 22
Greens Farms railroad station, 54
Grey, Henry, 72
Harvey, Alice, 18, 109
Hockanum house, 10
Hokinson, Helen, 10, 14, 109
Hubbell, Albert, 86, 96, 100, 102, 109
I Love Lucy, 42
I-95, 62, 76
Illustrators, 32
Jewish households, 58
Kemper Leather Works, 14
Krazy Vins, 94
Langner, Lawrence, 14, 48
Levitt Pavilion, 80
Lincoln, Abraham, 54
Lodge, John Davis, 76
Longshore golf course, 44, 72, 106
Main Street stores, 102
Marshall, Armenia, 14, 48
Mill Pond, 96
Minuteman statue, 52
Miramar nightclub, 8
Newman, Paul, 14, 18
Nike site, 30
NYNH&H Railroad, 46
Nyala Farms, 82
Obama, Barack, 54
Onion crop, 90
Pene du Bois, Guy, 44
Penguin apartments, 8
Picasso, Pablo, 74
Post Road, 86
Preston, David, 94, 109
Price, Garrett, 12, 28, 34, 40, 42, 44, 60, 74, 82, 109
Project Concern, 56
Railroad bridge, 36
Railroad station, 34, 46
Rally Round the Flag, Boys, 18, 30
Redford, Robert, 14
Ribicoff, Abe, 76
Rippe's Farm Market, 28
Rock & Roll bands, 26
Rockwell, Norman, 66
Roosevelt, Franklin D., 22, 70, 74
Saugatuck, 84
Saugatuck Congregational Church, 104
Saxon, Charles, 88, 98, 109
Serling, Rod, 42
Sherwood Diner, 94
Sherwood Island State Park, 98
Sherwood triplets, 40
Shulman, Max, 18, 30
Sondheim, Stephen, 48
Staples, William, 40
Stewart, Martha, 24
Television shows, 42
Temple Israel, 58, 104
Thomas, Marlo, 14
Twilight Zone, 42
Vanderbilt, Amy, 80
Von Langendorff, Baron, 10
Wakeman, Ned, 40
Wald, Lillian, 70
Washington, George, 38, 54
Westport Country Playhouse, 14, 48
Westport Public Library, 92
Westport Schools Permanent Art Collection, 74
Westport Town Seal, 38
Winslow, Richard Henry, 10
Woodward, Joanne, 14, 18
Works Progress Administration (WPA), 74
World War II, 22, 30, 58, 60, 108, 109
Wright Street building, 86
Yacht Clubs, 40